Islington
BOOK$WAP

Please take me home!
(better still, swap me with one of yours!)

Funny stories, sad stories, mystery stories,
scary stories, stories about school, stories
about friends, stories about animals, stories
about family. If you liked this story book,
we've got lots more like it that you can borrow
from our libraries!

Join your local Islington Library today!
www.islington.gov.uk/libraries

bug

braincell

cat

rabbits

slug

jellyfish

frog

triceratops

horse

cow

aardvark

bee

armadillo

rat

shark

elephant

sheep

snail

To Jake,
love from Mummy.
KD

First published in 1999 by
David Bennett Books Limited
United Kingdom.

BRITISH LIBRARY CATALOGUING IN PUBLICATION DATA
A catalogue record for this book is available from the British Library.

ISBN 1-85602-314-1

Printed in Singapore

The story of
cat

Created by bang on the door™

Illustrated by
Karen Duncan and Samantha Stringle

Story by
Jackie Robb and Berny Stringle

David Bennett Books

Cat was really scruffy
he always looked a mess,

He had no social graces,
table manners or finesse.

The posh cats found him funny
and asked him round to eat,

But once Cat got a sniff
of cream,
he'd wade in with both feet.

I don't care if he's your friend we're going home NOW

Now people who own posh cats, with class and pedigree,

won't let their pets be seen
with cats
who paddle in their tea.

So feeling like an outcast,
Cat sighed – and off he slunk

To seek advice from his old friend
the highly-scented Skunk.

"Tell me, Skunk, what's wrong
with me –
am I ugly, do I smell?"

Skunk just blushed bright red
and said,
"It's hard for me to tell!"

Hedgehog said, "Hey, looks don't count, it's who you are inside!"

But Cat would not be cheered up
and he crept off home to hide.

The posh cats rang him up again
and asked him out to play.

But their owners made them
stay indoors
and shooed poor Cat away.

"C'mon Cat!" said Hedgehog
"You've got puss-ibilities!

we could put you in that
posh cat show
if we fumigate your fleas."

"we'll comb your coat and dye
your fur
and manicure your claws.

Put curlers in your whiskers
and shine those dirty paws."

So spiffed up like the posh cats
Cat strutted at the show,

"Who is that magnifi-cat?"
the judges died to know.

The owners of the posh cats
seethed
to see Cat on the stage,

"What is Scruffy doing here?"
they shouted in a rage.

But the judges handed Cat
the cup
and Cat was pleased to win it,

'Coz the cup was filled with
double cream
and Cat just dived right in it!

bug

braincell

cat

rabbits

slug

jellyfish

frog

triCeratops

horse

cow

aardvark

bee

armadillo

rat

shark

elephant

sheep

snail